# ANCHORED

## *Five Keys To A Secure Faith*

# Dr. Steve McVey

# Copyright © 2014 Steve McVey

## *All Rights Reserved*

### ISBN-13: 978-1503326408
### ISBN-10: 1503326403

# TABLE OF CONTENTS

# INTRODUCTION
## Anchored In Life

I love being out on the water. The first time I went sailing I was so caught up in the euphoria of the experience that my wife, Melanie, and I decided to take sailing classes and become certified to sail alone. We did, and have enjoyed sailing many times since that first voyage years ago.

One of the first times that we sailed alone, we had gone from Nanny Cay on the island of Tortola in the British Virgin Islands to the tiny island of Marina Cay. Normally we would pick up a mooring ball at our destination so that we would tie off for the night, but on this occasion all of the mooring balls were already in use by other boats, making it necessary for us to drop anchor for the night.

It wasn't what I preferred to do because we were still novices, and setting an anchor requires a level of skill that ensures that the anchor holds. Otherwise it may drag or even completely pull loose, causing the boat to drift. Sleeping at night below deck while your boat drifts wherever the wind and current carries her is *not* a situation you want to find yourself in at any time. You don't want to suddenly wake up because you've run aground on a sand bar, run up onto a reef, or crashed into another boat. On that night at Marina Cay, my level of skill had never yet been put to the test.

One of the first things you learn about sailing is the importance of being securely anchored. That first time we spent the night out at anchor, I didn't sleep well. I couldn't, because I was afraid my anchor wouldn't hold. As the night ended it turned out that everything was fine but, because I didn't know that, I had hardly rested all night. I kept getting up all throughout the night to check the anchor's security on the bottom.

Many people's lives are like a boat at sea that isn't anchored. They're simply drifting through life and going wherever the current happens to carry them. They believe this about one thing and that about another. Ironically, their views often conflict with each other. For instance, they say they believe that God unconditionally forgives, but they also believe that He is a god of payback for wrongdoing if we don't meet certain conditions. Don't press them to explain this kind of inconsistency because they can't.

They aren't anchored in their beliefs about spiritual things or even in their personal circumstances. They can't rest because they are uneasy about where they might find themselves one day. They are like a boat being tossed around at sea with no way of knowing where it will end up or what the outcome will be. They spend their time without rest, trying to make sure that nothing bad is about to happen in life.

How much better it is to be anchored in life, to live with a sense of security that regardless of which direction the wind blows or how strong the current becomes, everything will be okay. Being anchored in life, like being anchored at sea, is the only way to rest at night and truly enjoy the journey during the day. Without inner rest, life loses its luster regardless how beautiful the scenery around you may actually be.

I have been a believer in Christ for over fifty years. I became a local pastor at the age of nineteen and served in that role for over twenty years. I resigned that position over twenty years ago and have been traveling the world sharing the gospel of grace since then. Over the past four decades I have counseled thousands of people on six continents, and across the time and distance I have seen one thing clearly: People are uneasy about their lives. Most are concerned about what may happen in the future and go to great lengths to try to avoid having anything painful come their way.

Many aren't even at peace about eternity. These often come from church environments where they learned a distorted view of God. They see Him first and foremost as a judge who carefully watches everything people do, and He isn't happy about what He sees most of the time. They compare their weakest moments of good behavior to their strongest misconceptions about a god they imagine who is rigid, stern and punitive and, as a result, they fear the worst. Some who have walked with Christ for years aren't even fully convinced that they will see Him when they die.

My own mother grew up in a denomination that taught her that her salvation could be lost if she didn't do the right things well enough and long enough to please God. She was taught that doing anything wrong might jeopardize her chance for heaven. Thankfully, she determined not to rear her children with that kind of fear.

She died in complete peace, having spent the day verbally expressing love to her family. "I hope I see angels" was one of the last things she said in her final hours as she approached death. So, in the end, all was well with her— not only spiritually, but even emotionally. But it wasn't always that way.

I remember having conversations with her many times through the years when we would talk about heaven and she would say, "I hope I make it."

"*Hope?*" I would ask incredulously. "Mom, you *know* you are trusting Jesus."

"Yes, I am," she would answer, "but I've not always been what I ought to be."

In those moments I would feel two things. I would feel thankful toward her for not allowing me to be taught about God in such a way that left me wondering whether He would receive me when the end comes. Secondly, I felt sorry for her that she had been abused by a stupid religious system that robbed her of the ability to simply rest in her faith, void of any worries about her Father's thoughts toward her.

My mother was a godly woman who loved Jesus Christ. Not perfect, but godly. It was the gap between the two that troubled her. The fact is that that gap exists in every one of us. There has only ever been One who behaved with consistent perfection at every moment. The rest of us can't make that claim. That's why we need grace.

## What Is Grace?

While the subject of grace has always been a topic of discussion among spiritually minded people, its popularity in recent years has gained momentum in a way that many of us believe to be unprecedented. From the spheres of New Age philosophy on one end to Christian Fundamentalism on the other, proponents of the concept are speaking about the subject as they understand it. Search online bookstores and you will find a plethora of resources that define it, describe it, and even specifically delineate how people's lives can be enhanced by accepting and applying grace to their daily lifestyle. Everybody from Buddhists to Baptists is talking about grace. Eastern religions, Christian denominations, motivational speakers, life coaches, mental health workers and countless others are increasingly using the word. Not only is the word gaining momentum in our society, it is becoming in vogue to use it.

When people from polar opposite perspectives like New Age teacher Eckhart Tolle and conservative Calvinist John MacArthur are both teaching people how to live in grace, any astute person quickly comes to understand that we can't all be talking about the same thing. You can be assured that you won't ever find these two speaking at the same conference together, despite the fact that both would affirm their personal commitment to what each calls "grace." I mention these two because they are well known men associated with teaching grace and they demonstrate what wide variance exists when it comes to an understanding of how the word is used.

How the subject is packaged and delivered depends on how the messenger defines it. To some, a grace-filled life is a compliant acceptance of whatever comes one's way. They see it as a life of nonresistance and absolute acceptance, and believe resistance to circumstances is the cause of suffering. They understand grace to be a state of being in which one has learned not only to yield to the universe but to gently participate with it in a way that brings personal growth.

To others, it means learning how to live a stringent lifestyle based on the guidelines they believe are enumerated in the Bible. Grace, to them, enables one to live up to the moral mandates prescribed by God; a lifestyle that stands in contrast to the cultural norm. To yet others, it means empowerment to be different from their surrounding environment and to zealously work to change the society around them. Far from being passive participants in the daily flow of circumstances, they see themselves as revolutionaries committed to resist and reshape their culture by the power that they too call "grace."

So when we use the word *grace,* it is shortsighted to assume that we are all using it in the same way. A common vocabulary doesn't always indicate that people are using the same dictionary. Words have meaning but that meaning must find a shared understanding if we are to accurately communicate what we want others to know. Even in Christian circles the word has become so common that it is incumbent upon those who are interested in the topic to consider what the word means to them. Is grace simply freedom from condemnation by God? Is it enablement to live by divine rules that one understands to be taught in the Bible? Is it simply having our sins forgiven? Is it empowerment to literally be a conduit of divine life in this world? Is it no more than

"God's Riches At Christ Expense," as the familiar acronym suggests? *What is grace?*

To define the word presents no small challenge. Not because grace is vague but rather because it is *vast*. The Apostle Peter referred to it as "the manifold grace of God." (See 1 Peter 4:10.) Some translations call it, "God's grace in its various forms" (*New International Version*) or "His great variety of spiritual gifts" (*New Living Translation*) or other similar descriptions. You get the point. The grace of God is multi-faceted, like a diamond with many facets. Hold it under the light in one way and you'll see a unique beauty. Then, when you slightly shift it under the light, it will take on a different yet equally beautiful appearance.

It is easier to describe grace than to define it. The reason for this fact is that the effect of grace in our lives depends on the area in which we appropriate it. Grace can relieve a guilty conscience. It can cause an abused, timid person to speak up and an obnoxious, overbearing person to shut up. It can empower one to stop bad behavior and simultaneously equip us for godly behavior. Grace can at times bring joy and at times deliver contrition. At times it can still us and at other times, stimulate zeal within us. Grace really is a one-size-fits-all answer for the human condition.

While the generic use of the word *grace* may be helpful in some contexts, the focus of our discussion here will be on its Original Source. Any time and any place that true grace can be found, you can be assured that you are seeing the presence of God. He alone is the fountainhead of authentic grace. Anything else is a shallow substitute.

The Apostle Paul began the New Testament books he wrote with a greeting of grace and peace. Greek culture so valued the concept of grace that Paul's salutation was the common one used when people greeted one another. People have always hungered for grace.

My bestselling book, *Grace Walk*, first published in 1995, has found wide acceptance around the world and has been translated into many languages. I believe the universal hunger for bona fide grace has played no small role in the success of that book. People are tired. They both need and want what grace can bring—a sense of contentment and confidence in their relationship to God that can only come when one knows that they are fully accepted by Him without any conditions. *My def of Grace*

We all instinctively know that we are here for a reason. We intuitively realize that there has to be more to life than sleeping eight hours a night, working eight hours a day, and then piddling away the other eight hours. Every human being has a destiny and we all sense that at some level.

For the purpose of this book, connecting the grace of God to the human condition leads to a working definition that will be used as a benchmark for the topics discussed here:

*Grace is the unconditional love of God toward us, through which He has embraced us and brought us into His very life.*

This book will show that the love of God for us is the basis of His actions toward us.

A life of grace is about living without fear as we take the journey through time that He has prepared for us. It is to live with the confidence that He is *for* us, and it is to live out the plan that He has for us in this world by the power of His indwelling Spirit. Grace is more than a nebulous and abstract concept reserved for mystical experiences and devotional reflection. It lives in the trenches of our daily lives, right along with us. It encourages us when we feel discouraged, empowers us when we feel weak, enlightens us when we are uncertain, equips us when we feel inadequate and, when we cooperate, engages with us in a way that will literally guide us into the successful fulfillment of the life plan our Creator designed for us.

Grace sounds like a person! There is good reason for that: Grace *is* a Person and His name is Jesus Christ. Remember the definition: Grace is the unconditional love of God toward us, through which He has embraced us and brought us into His very life. It is Grace Himself who lives *within us* and in whom we live. Grace walks out this life on planet earth each day with us. When we understand the implications of Grace living in and through us, it changes everything.

Perhaps the most wonderful aspect of grace is its unilateral nature. This one-sided divine intention to bless us is mind-boggling to anybody who begins to grasp it. Blessing from God without us having some part in gaining it? It's absurd in a world that swings on the hinges of reward and penalty.

The original biblical word translated as "grace" is the Greek word *charis,* and can also be rendered as "favor, blessing, or good will." It finds its source in the loving-kindness of our Father who has determined to pour out His love on us for no other reason than the fact that to do anything less would be a contradiction of His very nature. God is a good God who has determined to love us no matter what we do or don't do. His love isn't predicated on our good behavior or even our best efforts toward behaving well. *Agape* is love without conditions, not even one. Grace is the expression of that *agape* and is poured out on mankind whether we believe it, receive it, or even know it. It isn't given on the basis of how good we are but on how good God is.

## Grace Transforms Lives

When we know that and believe it, our lives will change. Some people think that spiritual change comes as the result of stressing God's judgment against sinful behavior, but that never has and never can bring real transformation to anybody's life. Some believe that change comes by learning rules from the Bible and then strenuously working toward keeping the rules we think we have found there, but nothing causes the very opposite outcome more than that approach. (See Romans 7:5.)

It isn't the fear of retribution or the following of rules that changes a person. The only thing that can bring authentic transformation to anybody is the love of God operating in our lives. The Apostle Paul wrote, "Don't you realize that it is God's kindness that is trying to lead you to Him and change the way you think and act?" (Romans 2:4, *God's Word Translation*). Examine that verse carefully, noting what it is that changes people's lives. Our lives are transformed when we learn how to rest in the loving acceptance of our God. It happens when we stop trying to achieve gaining His acceptance and just *receive* it by faith. That, and that alone, is the only thing that can change the way we think and act because receiving His love changes us from the inside-out, and that is the only way a real conversion can come.

A legalistic approach to life only affects the outside and that's as far as it goes. We can read the Bible with a cold heart. We can attend church services with a rotten attitude. We can give our money with ambivalence toward Him. There is much we can do outwardly that may look good to others, but God isn't impressed. His desire is to capture our hearts by His love because, once He has done that, He then completely has us—inside and out. While what we do outwardly has no inherent power to touch us inwardly, it is impossible to be inwardly transformed without our outward behavior being affected.

What does it look like when we are living a lifestyle transformed by grace? It looks like Jesus. He animates our behavior when we align our beliefs with grace. What we believe matters, because it is from our belief systems that we live our lives. Our beliefs affect how we relate to God.

However, grace is not only the conduit through which we experience God; it is also the pipeline to the world around us. What we believe about the grace of God will shape the way we relate to others, too. Our beliefs and our behavior are inseparable. In fact, it could be reasonably argued that behavior is an expression of our beliefs. That's why it is so important to believe the right thing. To believe wrongly about God and His grace is a sure way to fall short of our potential to relate both to Him and others in a healthy way.

Grace is the boat in which we are to live on this sea of life. We don't have to be tossed around by emotional fears and mental doubts about where we stand with God. There are anchors in the Good Ship Grace that will stabilize our lives in a way that we can live with confidence about our God's acceptance of us and about our standing with Him.

In the chapters that follow I am going to present you with five anchors that will transform your life. Accept these anchors and rest in their sufficiency, and you will find fear evaporating. You will experience a mind-shift that will bring a calm confidence to your life like you've never known. You will find an internal stability you may have never known. That's what anchors do. They keep the boat from being dangerously tossed around at sea.

Maybe, like my mother, you have been taught a concept of God that is wrong, and as a result you aren't experiencing the peace about life that you want to know. Will you open your heart and mind to receive truth that may be new to you as you read this book? I will intentionally cite many Bible verses in these chapters. I want you to see the biblical basis for what is here because some of it may contradict what you've been told in church. Which source will you believe—your tradition or your Bible? Are you willing to change your mind and embrace a new way of understanding?

These five anchors of grace will serve you well if you will utilize them. Sometimes people misquote Jesus by saying, "The truth will set you free." But that isn't what the verse says.

What Jesus actually said is, "You *will know the truth*, and the truth will make you free" (John 8:32, emphasis added). It's one thing to hear (or read) truth, and another to know it by believing it. Will you open your mind to consider truth that may be new to you? Many of us are steeped in the religious traditions of our pasts but to go forward in grace often requires that we rise above the place we have lived and take a fresh look at matters about which the Bible speaks.

There are many other important aspects of God's grace that we might consider but the scope of this book will discuss five biblical realities that are the anchors of the message of grace. Miss any of these and your boat of faith will be a rocky ride because the anchors aren't set in your life. Embrace the five truths that are discussed in this book and you will find yourself being transformed by a proper understanding of Him because, in the end, we all become like the god we understand. For good or for bad, how we perceive Him will affect every area of our lives. With that important fact in mind, let us consider the first anchor.

# CHAPTER ONE
## The Anchor of the Trinity

The most fundamental element of living in grace is a proper concept of God. To get this one wrong is like rounding the bases and touching home plate only to discover that you didn't touch first base. Whatever else we may do makes little difference if we have a wrong concept of who God is. What you believe about Him will leave no area of your life untouched.

Theology, at its core, is what we believe about God and every person has a theological viewpoint, whether they know it or not. If you hear somebody say they don't care about theology, their statement reveals their lack of understanding of the word. Everybody has a theology because the word refers to what we believe about God, and not only do we all have a belief about Him but what we believe about God will shape our attitudes and actions more than anything in life.

Belief in a god who despises those who oppose him and who sees them as infidels who need to be destroyed is what caused some to savagely massacre thousands of innocent people while they worked in their offices on September 11, 2001. Belief in a God who loves every person, including the last, the lowest and the least, caused another to give her life to living with lepers in Calcutta, where she showed love to them in practical ways that made an immediate difference. One's belief about God has huge impact on how she lives her life.

The effect of our concept of God doesn't always influence us in such dramatic ways as these. Sometimes the understanding that a person has about God can be seen more subtly. It may be an underlying attitude of judgmentalism toward those we believe are misbehaving. On the other hand, it could be a posture of loving acceptance toward those whose actions don't align with our own belief system. Make no mistake about it—how you see God will influence how you see people. You'll see them the way you consciously or subconsciously think He sees them.

## Our God Is a Relational God

While it's true that mere mortals can't understand everything about an Eternal God, there are many things that we can know of His nature. All that can be known of God is the result of His self-disclosure to us. In other words, we know what He has chosen to tell us and to show us. No more and no less. We don't figure this out on our own. The good news is that God has chosen to reveal Himself to us in ways that are life-altering when we grasp them.

The very first thing the Bible reveals about Him is that He exists as a triune being. He is the Three-In-One God. When Genesis 1:1 says, "In the beginning, God," we are immediately notified of the trinitarian nature of God. The word *God* is the Hebrew word, *Elohiym*. The word is plural, denoting the fact that He doesn't abide alone. There is a plurality in His very essence. The first time He is mentioned in Scripture, the thing God chose to show us about Himself was His triune nature. Don't underestimate the importance of this.

Although the word *trinity* wasn't used until Tertullian coined the term in the late second century, the concept is taught in the Bible from the very first verse. The reason for discussing this doctrinal tenet first is because the Trinity is the exact expression of the very essence of God. If we miss or even marginalize the triune nature of God, it will be impossible to rightly and clearly articulate anything else that we may say about Him. How can we be correct in any aspect of understanding Him if we come from a completely wrong starting assumption?

Some have grappled with why this emphasis on the Trinity is so important to the Christian faith. One answer is that the Trinity makes clear the most important aspect of God that can be known about Him: *God is relational.* He does not and cannot exist apart from relationship. Don't quickly read past this paragraph without internalizing its meaning and importance. *God is relational.* He is more concerned about sharing His life with others than anything else. This may be the most important thing you will ever believe about God.

Why did Jesus come into this world? He answered, "I have come *so that they might have life* and have it to the fullest" (John 10:10, emphasis added). The incarnation of Jesus Christ is first and foremost about God coming to us to share His life with us. When Adam was created in the Garden of Eden, He "breathed into his nostrils the breath of life;

and man became a living being" (Genesis 2:7). God gave life to Adam for a reason. He wanted to include humanity in the Circle of Love that had always existed among the Father, Son and Holy Spirit.

Read the Genesis narrative and you will find that God didn't create Adam and Eve, give them their assignments and then head back to heaven with the knowledge that His work was done. Our loving Creator made us to joyfully share His life with us. He isn't interested in separation from those He created and loves. In fact, He has refused to allow separation. He made us to live in union with Him and to find our very lives in Him. More than anything else, God wants us to know and enjoy Him. The 17th century church reaffirmed this in the Westminster Confession saying, "Man's chief end is to glorify God and to enjoy Him forever." It isn't without importance that glorifying God and enjoying Him are linked in this commonly accepted confessional statement.

You may wonder why I am putting forward this emphasis on the relational aspect of God's nature. "Of course God is relational," you may think. "Don't we all know that?"

The answer to that question is yes and no. Yes, we understand at an intellectual level that God is interested in having a relationship with each of us. On the other hand, no, most of us don't really understand the implications of the relational aspect of His nature.

### Rejecting the Courtroom Deity

Ask the average person to tell you what is most important in the day-to-day relationship they have to God and few will say that "to enjoy Him" is the "chief end" of their lives. Reveling in the love of God probably won't make most people's list of how to glorify Him. You'll more likely get an answer that has to do with obeying Him or serving Him or something else works-related. When we frame our relationship to God in terms of what we do, we will inevitably come to the place where we ask ourselves, "How well am I doing?" The very question then becomes a bridge that we can easily cross, leading us to a skewed understanding of who He is and why we have a relationship to Him.

When our focus is more oriented toward our behavior than it is toward Him, imagining Him judging our actions to see how well we're doing becomes inescapable. It is at this very point that we move away from seeing our Father as primarily relational and begin to see him as the god who is judicial. He becomes (in our minds) the Judge who watches what we do, scrutinizing our actions to make sure that they are up to par. When we take that step, it may seem like a small shift but in reality we have just moved away from grace and into legalism.

Doesn't God care what we do? Do our actions not matter to Him? Of course He cares about our behavior, and actions do matter. The question is *why* do they matter?

Certainly, it's not because God is the morality monitor of the cosmos whose job it is to make sure that we're all behaving like we are supposed to. No, behavior matters because actions have consequences. Our God loves us and doesn't want to see us make choices that lead us to harm. He doesn't want to see us hurt ourselves, and *that* is the reason He cares about our actions. He loves us and His relationship to us motivates Him to guide us in how we behave lest we bring harm to ourselves.

God didn't tell Adam not to eat from the Tree of the Knowledge of Good and Evil to be selfish and hold out on something Adam might enjoy. He forbade the first couple to eat from the tree because they would die if they ate from it! God loved them and didn't want to see them suffer the consequences of disobeying Him by eating its fruit.

The Trinity is a culture of loving acceptance and you are loved and accepted regardless of how you behave. His heart is linked to ours through love, not laws of performance. However, our Triune God desires for you to avoid bringing harm to yourself by ignoring what He has instructed about how to live. If we choose to disobey, we will suffer the consequences, but even then He will walk through the pain with us. He will comfort and guide us as we move through the injury we have brought upon ourselves. He won't be saying, "I told you so" or "This is what you get for not listening to me." Instead, He will sweep you up into His arms and say, "Let me carry you. Just trust me. I'll carry you through this." That is what a relational God does!

Reject the idea of a judicial god who judges your life while looking for an infraction of the rules. That is not who He is. He is interested in redemption and restoration, not retribution. Christ Jesus is not a courtroom judge. He came to deliver us from sin's penalty, not to impose it on us. Don't confuse your relational God who revealed Himself in

Jesus for a judicial god who is more in
in rules than relationships.

A relational God would do everything
necessary to show Adam that he was still loved
and accepted after he sinned in the Garden of
Eden. He would come to Adam, in pursuit of
him, even though he had sinned. He would
promise him that sin would not get the last
word over humanity.

He would cover him with the skin of an
animal like a man gives a beautiful diamond
engagement ring to the one he pledges to
make his own forever. He would put him out
of the Garden to protect him from himself, lest
he eat from the Tree of Life and, in so doing,
damn and doom himself to a place beyond
redemption by becoming eternally trapped in
his fallen estate. He would go with Adam
when he left the Garden of Eden and would be
with him all his life, loving him until He led
him safely home.

A judicial god would have made Adam
seek Him; He'd wait for him to beg for

forgiveness. He would be angry and punitive. He would make Adam prove his sorrow about having sinned by changing his ways and gradually regaining that god's acceptance and favor.

Do you see the difference between the relational God revealed in the Trinity and the judicial god manufactured in the murky minds of the misinformed? It's one thing to say we believe that God is relational but what we believe becomes clear when we apply our understanding to our own lives and the lives of others.

A relational God wouldn't keep score or, to quote another who understood God better than most of us: He would be "patient and kind. He does not envy, does not boast, and is not proud. He does not dishonor others, is not self-seeking; He is not easily angered and He keeps no record of wrongs. He does not delight in evil but rejoices with the truth. He always protects, always trusts, always hopes, always perseveres." (See 1 Corinthians 13.)

A judicial god would have rejected Abraham when, because of fear, he had his wife go into Pharaoh's tent to sleep with him. The relational God didn't shame him but only reaffirmed the covenant He had sworn to him earlier.

A judicial god would have had the prodigal son's father lecture him. The relational God had him laugh with joy over the son and throw a party in his honor. A judicial god would have had the father leave the self-righteous older brother in the outer darkness alone while everybody else partied. The relational God had his dad go out into the outer darkness with him, refusing to leave him there alone.

A judicial god would have told a parable where the vineyard owner paid people what they deserved for working in his field. The relational God told the story in a way that the owner lavished generosity on everybody, regardless of how long they had worked.

Do you get the picture? Example after example from Scripture could be cited to illustrate the fact that it's all about relationship to God. The Trinity is the matrix for the family system that our God desired for all humanity. His eternal intention was to include us in the Circle of Love and Life that has eternally existed among the Godhead.

Before the first tick of the clock He had already embraced us and cuddled us in the center of the circle of the Father, Son and Spirit. Paul wrote, "Even before He made the world, God loved us and chose us in Christ to be holy and without fault in His eyes" (Ephesians 1:4, *NLT*). When did this happen? "Before He made the world," the Bible says. Where were you when He chose you? "In Christ," the Scripture clearly affirms.

The inside story the gospel tells is that you were in before you knew it. The game is rigged. Before sin stained the garment of humanity, the Eternal Eradicator had already cleansed the stain by "the Lamb slain from the foundation of the world" (Revelation 13:8, *King James Version*). Sin was a big issue in time, but in the eternal realm nobody experienced the slightest nervousness about it because there was the Lamb, having drawn the consequence of sin into Himself before it even became a problem in time. We might say that we were all born with a credit—a big credit. Our sin was already forgiven before we even got here to commit the first one. It was that important to God. *Nothing* was going to keep us from living in His loving embrace. He saw to that.

If you want your relationship to your Heavenly Father to be one that causes you to experience the abundant life that He created you to know, renounce the lie that He relates to you as a courtroom judge and begin to renew your mind to the fact that He relates to you as your *Abba,* the word Jesus used that denotes the kind of childlike relationship that a baby has to its daddy.

*Living Inside the Circle Of Love*

Your place in the Circle of Life and Love is as secure as the place of Jesus because you are in Him. The only way you could be expelled is if the Father and the Holy Spirit decide to evict Jesus. This very explanation is absurd to the point of stupidity because our God is one indivisible essence expressed in three Persons. There can be no separation between the three, or God would cease to exist. God the Father, God the Son and God the Holy Spirit have brought you into an irrevocable union with Himself through your adoption in Jesus Christ. One could easier remove all the salt from all the oceans of the world than we can be removed from the union we share with the Trinity. We could make all the stars across the night sky turn black before we could cause our God to turn back on His decision to eternally love us.

The doctrine of the Trinity is a necessary anchor in life because, when we see that relationship, we see our place of origin. We see our home. We see that we are included and that we always have been.

This recognition of reality doesn't just affect the way we see ourselves in relationship to God. It transforms the way we see others, too. Unless you believe that the God who is pure love by His very essence willfully chose to exclude some people and reject others, it becomes very apparent that we all stand on equal ground when it comes to His disposition toward us. "For God so loved *the world* that He gave His only begotten Son," the Bible assures us.

This relationship between Deity and humanity doesn't suggest that everybody is a Christian, but it does prove that there is nothing left for God to do for us. He has already done it all. Through Jesus He has drawn us into Himself, and the only thing left for us to do is to say, "Thank you!" The Judge of the Cosmos has judged you to be a precious treasure to Him. He doesn't see you for what you've done but as the person He created you to be. He sees you for who you truly are—His beloved child! He has taken away the sin that held mankind in slavery and brought us safely home. (See John 1:29, 1 John 3:5, 1 Peter 2:24.)

Our Triune God embraced us in eternity past. Later, like a fatal disease, sin broke out on planet earth but the Antidote to Sin had already cured the cancer in eternity. Its application in time took place at Golgotha, and ever since then we can all rest in absolute peace because, as Jesus said, "It is finished." The Father was "in Christ reconciling the world to Himself" (2 Corinthians 5:19) when "through the eternal Spirit (He) offered Himself" (Hebrews 9:14). There is the gospel message of the Trinity at work to save us from the certain death that sin brings. Through the joint effort of the Father, Son and Spirit, the cancer of sin has gone into remission. Now we simply need to believe it and experience it! (See Acts 2:38, Acts 10:43, Luke 24:47.)

The finished work of the cross makes it possible for us to look at every human being as a precious object of God's affection. If Jesus loves the world, and He does, and if our

Triune God proved His love at the cross, and He did, then that reality will change the way we relate to people—to *all* people. If nobody is excluded by Pure Love, the implications of how that affects our lifestyles are staggering.

# CHAPTER TWO
## The Anchor of Love

Once we are anchored in the realization that God isn't a Judge sitting in a courtroom assessing guilt and passing sentence on humanity but instead that He is our Heavenly Daddy in a living room who invites us to enjoy sitting on His lap, we are moving to a place where we can begin to understand His true character. When asked to identify the most preeminent characteristic of God, many people would say that God is holy. While it is true that God is holy, the meaning of that statement isn't what some people think.

Some believe the holiness of God is a sort of divine cleanliness that is so sterile that the very presence of sin causes Him to recoil from us because, after all, who among us hasn't sinned at times? That idea is as far from what it means to say that God is holy as one can get. God doesn't pull back from sin's presence. To the contrary, in the incarnation He has proven His passion to rush *toward* people trapped in sin so that He can take it away from us and set us free to live the life He created us to enjoy. Jesus stepped into a world filled with sin and then spent His whole ministry seeking out those who were still deeply mired in it so that He could free them from it.

The holiness of God speaks to the fact that He is "in a class of His own." The word means "to be set apart." In other words, God isn't like us. His thoughts are not our thoughts and His ways are not our ways. (See Isaiah 55:8.) God once said, "You thought that I was just like you" (Psalm 50:21) but the point is He isn't. We have projected our darkened perception about who He is onto Him based on the way we have felt about ourselves and others, and the result has been catastrophic. We have ended up believing in a god whose greatest obsession is that we do the right thing by avoiding sin, but that is *not* what God is about at the core of His being. As we learned in the last chapter, our Triune God is about relationships not rules. He is infinitely more interested in people than He is in their performance.

Starting from the place where we understand that He is relational, we are better able to grasp *why* God is so interested in relationship. The reason is simple: God is love. This anchoring truth of the love of God is the catalyst for everything. We could have as easily begun this book by discussing God as Love and then have shown how He is relational as a result of that love. I began with the Trinity because the relational aspect of His identity is the first thing revealed in Scripture, in Genesis 1:1.

The fact is that the relational aspect of God and the aspect of His love are actually inseparable. He is relational precisely because He *is* love. If anybody ever asks you to describe God, the first word you speak needs to be the word *love*. To say that God is love is to speak the greatest reality that we can know of Him. To say such a thing is more than we can say about anybody else. Others may act loving but God *is* love. There is nothing more foundational about who He is than that. If one were to describe God without talking about love, they know no more about Him than my dog, Emma, understands about quantum physics. Love isn't just something God does. It is who He is. Nothing God does can ever originate from any place that contradicts love, or He would be acting in contradiction to His own character.

## Is God Part Love Or Pure Love?

If you find yourself not so sure about that last statement, take another look at it. Is God pure love or not? Some people argue that love is simply one part of His character and that there are others which deserve equal place in describing Him. What they are suggesting is that God isn't pure love but is only part love. Their view is that He is part love and part other things. They believe that characteristics like holiness, justice, and wrath belong to another side of God that somehow contrasts to His love. Such an idea impugns the character of God. There is no other side to God. Jesus was the exact representation of His Father and He revealed nothing about a legalistic god who was obsessed with people's behavior over their well-being. (See Hebrews 1:3.) Humans conjured up that god from our own sense of guilt and shame. Jesus showed us that we've had it all wrong. God isn't like that—not at all.

God isn't a multiple personality who at times is one of love and at other times is something else that completely opposes love. Everything that can be understood about Him must be interpreted in the light of His love. This is the anchor of true Christianity. Love isn't one piece of the pie. It is the crust that holds all the other pieces in place.

God's love isn't called forth by inherent virtue in us that convinces Him to love us. The opposite is the case. His abundantly loving nature caused Him to bestow great value on us by virtue of the fact that He loves us. You are loved by God and that gives you great value!

Does this conflict with His holiness? Not at all. His love is an expression of His holiness, in a class by itself. To attempt to impose a human paradigm of love on God is to reduce it to a whimsical emotion. People sometimes stop loving. A man becomes involved with a younger woman at work and, like a tender plant suddenly drenched with weed killer, his wife's love for him may completely wither and die. Betrayed by a trusted friend, we may find that love is replaced by cold ambivalence. Natural human love can go away under the right circumstances.

The greatest love you will ever know from another human being is, at best, tentative. Despite the promises of poetry and song, human love can wither and die but not Divine

Love. God loves you. The words have been spoken so many times by so many people that there is the danger that they have lost their edge, like a worn-out blade that no longer has the ability to cut.

The emotions that accompany human love may wax and wane but God promises, "I, the LORD, do not change" (Malachi 3:6). "For the LORD is good; His loving kindness is everlasting and His faithfulness to all generations" (Psalm 100:5). God loves you and He will never change His mind. His love for you isn't stronger at some times than it is at others. It is constant, without wavering.

You may fall down, give up, turn your back, or just decide you've had enough of living in faith. But even when we have no faith in Him, He is still faithful to us. (See 2 Timothy 2:13.) His love is constant and nothing you do or don't do is going to change that fact. People may tire of our deficiencies, our irritating ways and our self-centeredness, and they may give up on us. But God loves us and He's not going to give up on us, no matter what.

Although the love of God is the anchor of life, it is also the hardest thing people struggle to truly believe and accept. Trapped in the shallow waters of natural love, many people simply cannot see the vast ocean of divine affection with its waves of supernatural agape billowing over them.

"But what if I were to turn my back on God and renounce Him? Surely you aren't suggesting that He would still love me!"

"How can you believe that God could still love somebody who committed that sin?"

"Yes, God loves us... but you can take this too far. After all, what we do still matters to God!"

Thus goes the litany of objections to divine love. Maybe you struggle with your own questions. Maybe you can't reconcile certain things you believe to be true with this whole concept of a kind of divine love that is immeasurable, unconditional and irrevocable. Maybe it seems like it's overdoing it to stress God's love to such an extreme. It just doesn't make sense!

I'm on the same side of the line as you are. There are aspects of God's love that I don't understand either. His love is too big for me to get my arms around and mentally manage. As hard as I've tried, I can't sort it all out. I still have unanswered questions about His love.

However, I have embraced this anchor and it continues to transform my life. I have chosen to apprehend what I can't comprehend. I refuse to allow my limited ability to understand God's unlimited love to insulate me from enjoying it. Yes, there are still unresolved questions. We all have questions, but until we get the answers, why not choose to believe in His love and receive it as something bigger and better than anything we've ever known? This God of Love is outrageous to human sensibilities.

He is the Father who falls on the neck of returning prodigals and, with tears of joy streaming down His cheeks, kisses them and shouts with laughter, "My son is home! Let's have a party." (See Luke 15:20-24.) He is the Mother who smothers Her babies in kisses as they snuggle against Her breasts. (See Psalm 131:2.) He is the Artist who points to you and declares proudly to the universe, "Look what I made!" (See Ephesians 2:10.) He is the Composer who sings love songs to you. (See Zephaniah 3:17.) He is the Wealthy Merchant who sold everything He had so that He could make you His own. (See Matthew 13:45-46.) He is the King of kings and Lord of lords who left the glory of His exalted throne in heaven, waded through the filth of this sinful world, and descended into the hellish horror of taking your sin upon Himself—all for one simple reason. He looked beyond the horror and saw you standing on the other side, waiting for Him to rescue you.

With the kiss of grace He awakened you from your sleep of spiritual death. He swept you off your feet and is now carrying you toward the eternal honeymoon home He has prepared for you. (See John 14:2-3.) Having conquered death and hell, nothing stands in His way. Nothing will deter Him from His mission. (See Daniel 4:35.)

The marriage feast has been prepared. The table has been set. You stand in the corridor of time at the place where the door of eternity is about to swing open to receive you. Just beyond the door is singing. It is a great multitude of wedding guests who have anxiously awaited your arrival. As you soon step across the boundary from time into eternity, you will hear their song:

*Hallelujah! For the Lord our God, the Almighty reigns!*

*Let us rejoice and be glad and give the glory to Him,*

*for the marriage of the Lamb has come and His bride*

*has made herself read.* (Revelation 19:6-7)

Your life story has a happy ending, so it only makes sense to relax in the meantime. Trust Him and receive His love and then rest in faith that He has everything under control. He has achieved what He wanted to do, which is to bring you into union with Himself. There's nothing left for us to achieve. The only thing we need to do is believe and receive the good news—receive *Him*—by faith.

## The Outgoing Tide

Once we have understood and accepted God's love for us, we find ourselves wanting to touch the lives of others in the same way. It isn't something we see ourselves as having to do, but it is a normal response to the divine love we ourselves have experienced. It's as if the Tide of Love carries us out to the world where we can share His life with others. John said, "as He is, so are we in this world" (1 John

4:17). The great privilege we have is to express Christ to others. We become more than servants. We begin to live as sons who go about our Father's business, living and loving on His behalf. (See Galatians 4:7.)

The focus of the Christian world today is largely on the subject of how to live, but our attention should be on learning to love others just as we are loved by Him. Empty religion is preoccupied with correct behavior defined by doing the right things and avoiding the wrong ones. The lifeblood of an authentic expression of faith in Christ is loving people the way He does. Behavior can be elevated no higher than that.

Is not the fundamental purpose of the relationships we have with others to express the love of our God to them? According to Jesus, it is. He told His disciples that He had come so that they might know the love of God in the way He had always known it. He prayed to His Father in John 17:4, "I glorified You on the earth, having accomplished the work which You have given me to do."

What was the work that God the Father gave Him to do? It was to make the Father's love known to us. His mission was to cause us to see and experience the love of God. On His last night in this world before being crucified, while praying to His Father, Jesus said these words in the presence of His disciples:

*In the same way you gave me a mission in the world, I give them a mission in the world.* I'm consecrating myself for their sakes so they'll be truth consecrated in their mission. I'm praying not only for them, but also for those who will believe in me because of them and their witness about me. *The goal is for all of them to become one heart and mind—just as you, Father, are in me and I in you. So they might be one heart and mind with us.* Then the world might believe that you, in fact, sent me. The same glory you gave me, I gave them. So they'll be as unified and together as we are—I in them and you in me. Then they'll be mature in this oneness and give the godless world evidence that you've sent me and loved them in the same way you've loved me.

Father, I want those you gave me to be with me, right where I am. So they can see my glory, the splendor you gave me, having loved me long before there ever was a world. Righteous Father, the world has never known you, but I have known you and these disciples know that you sent me on this mission. I have made your very being known to them—who you are and what you do—and continue to make it known so that your love for me might be in them exactly as I am in them.

(John 17:28-26, *The Message*, emphasis added)

Jesus asked His Father to cause those who believe in Him to give the world we live in evidence that the same love God has for Jesus is inside each of us. That is our "mission in the world," given to us by Jesus Christ Himself.

When our lives are an expression of the union we share with the Father, Son and Holy Spirit, what will be expressed will be a supernatural, unequivocal, unconditional, irrevocable, and indiscriminate outpouring of love on everybody else. This is the natural result of realizing how deeply we are loved by Him. 1 John 4:19 says, "we love because He first loved us." We don't just love Him for that reason. We love everybody for that reason. We cannot completely experience His love without then expressing it.

There is a sense in which we become Jesus to others. I don't mean to imply that we become deified, but that His life being expressed through us becomes so predominant that others see Him when they look at us.

What does it look like when we live this life? It looks like Jesus! He loved the down-and-outers (the Samaritan woman) and the up-and-outers (Matthew). He loved the unrighteous (Zaccheus) and the self-righteous (Saul of Tarsus). He loved the rogues (Peter) and the religious (Nicodemus). He loved the horribly immoral (the woman taken in adultery) and the highly moral (the rich young ruler). Jesus just loved.

He didn't get the seal of approval from the religious world of His day for one simple reason—He didn't meet their religious expectations. They didn't like that kind of love, and still don't. If you go around just loving everybody, you may invoke the same disapproval from the self-righteous of our day. The hollow world of religion may talk about love but they are, in fact, very discriminating about whom they will and won't love.

Jesus often got Himself into trouble with the religious crowd for showing love to the wrong people. The consensus of the religious leaders was, "This man accepts sinners and even eats with them" (Luke 15:2). It's ironic how that Jesus repelled the hyper-religious while attracting the very people they rejected. Follow the steps of Jesus through the New Testament and you will find Him loving the immoral, the ignorant, the poor and the lepers—those who were the social rejects of the elite and sophisticated Roman Empire in which He lived. You need to know that Jesus hasn't changed since then.

The Apostle Peter said that you have now become a participant in the divine nature of Jesus Christ. (See 2 Peter 1:4.) To love profusely is the normal way of life for a grace-walker. Jesus said that it is "by this (that) all men will know you are My disciples, if you have love for one another" (John 13:25). Because you have the spiritual DNA of Jesus Christ and His is the same as His Father's, and if the very essence of God is love... you get the point. It isn't hard to connect the dots here. It is your nature to love. It's that simple.

Having been touched by Agape, we find ourselves sensing an increasing desire to share His love with others. Nobody has to insist that we share the gospel with people. We are like the early disciples who said, "we cannot stop speaking about what we have seen and heard" (Acts 4:20). Nobody has to scold or shame us into caring about people. We can't do otherwise. We love because He loves us with such an intensity that we can't keep it to ourselves. We don't want to keep it to ourselves!

Here's a radical idea: Let's act like Jesus, even if the Pharisees don't like it. Let's just love people indiscriminately. Let's love them whether they're pimps or preachers—whether they are crack-heads or corporate heads—whether they are drug addicts or deacons, whether they are immoral or moral. Let's just love them all!

Our God-given goal is simply to reveal His love to others. If we began to accept people wherever they are and love them the way Christ loves them, we might be surprised by what happens in their lives. While we certainly don't condone sinful behavior, we must remember that we are to express the love of the one "who came not into the world to condemn the world, but that the world through Him might be saved" (John 3:17). We neither condemn nor condone those who sin. We just love them as God loves them.

Love people. Just love them. Love them radically. You don't have to offer an opinion about everything everybody else does. Just love them. You don't have to condone or condemn them. Just love them. Love them when they don't deserve it. Love them if they act responsibly or repulsively.

Let's love people to the point that some won't understand it and the Pharisees will think it is shameful. When we love that way, we are in good company and, if you listen carefully, you may hear a still, small voice whisper, "I'm so proud of you. You look and act just like Me! Now, together let's love the world."

# CHAPTER THREE
## The Anchor of Inclusion

When we consider the gospel of Jesus Christ we must answer the question, "For whom was the gospel given?" Did He come to rescue everybody or just some people? On the night that Jesus was born, a heavenly messenger appeared in the night sky and answered that question: "I bring you good news of great joy which will be for *all* the people; for today in the city of David there has been born for you a Savior, who is Christ the Lord" (Luke 2:10-11,emphasis added). There is no doubt then that Jesus came for all people. Nobody was left out when the angel made this announcement to the shepherds. Jesus was born into this world for *all* people.

What about His death? Did He die only for an elect minority while the rest were excluded or does what He did on the cross also include every person? Again, the Bible gives a clear answer in Hebrews 2:9: "But we see Jesus, who was made a little lower than the angels for the suffering of death, crowned with glory and honor; that he by the grace of God should *taste death for every man.*" Was what Jesus did on the cross for *every* person or not? This Bible verse plainly says that He died for *every* person.

When Jesus took the sinful human condition to the cross, who died with Him? The Apostle Paul "concluded this, that one died for all, therefore all died" (2 Corinthians 5:14). Obviously, the one who died was Jesus. For whom did He die? Paul says it was for *all* that Jesus died. Then he goes on to say in the same sentence, "therefore *all* died." Is it the same "all" who died with Christ as the "all" for whom He died? Of course it is and to think otherwise is absurd. Jesus died for every sinner in Adam and every sinner in Adam died with Jesus. Adam's race died. How many of them? *All,* claims the Apostle Paul.

Every person became a sinner because of their association with Adam. Romans 5:12 says, "Therefore just as sin came into the world through one man, and death through sin, and so death spread to all men because all died." The death that came to mankind through Adam was universal. Nobody was exempt.

Four verses later in the same chapter in Romans: "And the free gift is not like the result of that one man's sin. For the judgment following one trespass brought condemnation but the free gift following many trespasses brought justification" (Romans 5:16). The evil deed of Adam included everybody. All were included in it and in the condemnation that followed. Then the Bible says that "the free gift following many trespasses brought justification." Adam's deed brought condemnation to everybody. Christ's deed brought justification to everybody—the same ones who had been affected by Adam. This isn't a difficult concept if we simply accept what the Bible teaches. Just like what Adam did rendered every person unrighteous (a sinner) so what Jesus died has rendered every person justified. None of us had to do anything, including believe it, for the result of Adam's sin to connect to us. In the same way, what Jesus did affects us whether we believe it or not.

But wait, here's where some people get confused. The next verse says, "For if, because of one man's trespass, death reigned through that one man, much more will *those who receive* the abundance of grace and the free gift of righteousness reign in life through the one man Jesus Christ" (Romans 5:17). "There!" some will argue. "We *do* have to receive His grace and the gift that makes us righteous!" Yes, we do. You'll find no argument here that suggests we must not believe and receive

Jesus by faith. The question is what happens when we do?

The same people who argue that people are already sinners even before they commit their first sin in life turn right around and argue that people aren't righteous until they believe and receive Christ. Do you see the inconsistency? They contend that what Adam did affected everybody even before they did a single thing to experience that reality. How then can these same ones argue that what Jesus did doesn't affect people until and unless they first do something, namely believe?

### Everybody Was Included In Adam And In Jesus

The answer isn't hard to see when we look at Adam. His action brought sin to the human race. That was an objective fact whether people knew it or not. When a person became old enough to commit a sin for the first time, he was simply experiencing something at that point in time that had already been true of him. In the same way, faith in Christ doesn't cause us to be justified. We are justified because "the free gift following many trespasses brought justification." The fact of justification is that everybody is included in what Jesus did just like all were included in what Adam did. We believe to *experience* it, not to make it happen. It is the cross, not our commitment, that makes it real.

Lest there be any confusion about it, Paul takes an unequivocal, unambiguous stand on the issue in Romans 5:18 when he writes, "Therefore, as one trespass led to condemnation for all men, so *one act of righteousness leads to justification and life for all men*" (emphasis added). This verse clearly points to the objective aspect of justification for every single person for whom Christ died. That leaves nobody out. We must believe to experience it but whether we believe it or not, Jesus has done what He has done for mankind, and no lack of faith on our part negates the success of the cross and turns it into a failure.

If you have been indoctrinated to believe that we are only included when we believe in Christ, I ask you to consider that you are assigning greater impact to the sinful act of Adam than to the righteous act of Jesus Christ. Does it make sense that what the first Adam did affected every person apart from their acknowledgement of his action but what the Last Adam did only affects those who acknowledge and have faith in Him and His work? If that were so, wouldn't it make the first Adam's work more powerful than the work of Jesus, the Last Adam? This says nothing about what *we* do with His work. It simply speaks to the level of success of what Jesus did as the Last Adam.

Adam's act in the Garden didn't cause humanity to become *potential* sinners, based on how they responded to what He did. In him, being sinners became an actual reality for every person. They neither had to believe it nor even know it.

In the same way, the righteous act of Jesus didn't create the *potential* for justification. No, Paul plainly says that his act brought "justification and life for *all* men." Again, you may have been taught differently in the past. If so, your mind may be racing to verses you are familiar with that seem to suggest something different from what Romans 5 teaches. The question I challenge you to answer is, "What are you going to do with the clear teaching of Romans chapter five?"

It is likely that many of the verses that come to your mind that seem to contradict what I have laid out here from the Apostle Paul's letter to the Romans are texts that speak about experiential, subjective matters. There is no contradiction between those verses and these. They are speaking of subjective experience, and Romans 5 is speaking about objective facts which are true whether we do or don't experience them. We *do* need to believe. We must receive the gospel by faith. That is the only way we can experience its benefits. However, we believe it because it is *already* true and not so that it can become true. The success of Jesus's work on the cross isn't up to us. When He said, "It is finished," He meant it. He didn't say, "Your move."

There are teachers speaking falsely who will tell you that this message of inclusion is dangerous. They will advise you that this teaching is veiled Universalism and suggests that everybody is going to heaven, whether they believe on Christ or not. They will suggest that the very word *inclusion* is a heretical word. Don't believe it.

Which concept of God do you have? Is He a god who excludes people from the beginning? Is he a god who has done his best to reach humanity but can't know for sure whether his effort is a success or not until we let him know by making our decision? Is he a god who couldn't do something that at least equaled what Adam did when he affected the whole human race by his actions?

These teachers will use words like *hyper-grace,* as if to suggest that we can overstate God's grace and make it sound better than it is. They will build straw men arguments and then tear down the arguments that they falsely claim that grace teachers are saying. They will take the words of others out of context and, in doing so, will change the original meaning of the statements they quote. They will twist the words of those who teach the message of grace and try to convince you that those grace teachers are leading people into error.

Then, based on that fear they have instilled into you, they will try to scare you into not thinking for yourself as you prayerfully study the Bible and ask the Holy Spirit to teach you. They will call this "a new teaching" for the simple reason that it is new *to them.* They will make "free will" the god of all things by implying that the human will isn't influenced and often even controlled by the input we have received into our minds throughout life. (Do you seriously think that a Muslim child in Iran has the same "free will" to choose Christ that a child reared in a Christian home in North America possesses?)

Oh yes, the critics of pure grace are out there, and they work overtime to keep you from this glorious truth. For the most part, they aren't consciously trying to be sinister. They are motivated by fear and, in panic, they strike out accordingly.

Is their projection of god the one you believe in right now? Or do you believe in the Triune God whose very essence is love? If you believe that God is the one described so far in this book, then you must conclude, as did the Apostle Paul, that He is an inclusive God who has embraced everybody and left out no one.

You will recognize that, although some reject Christ and might even reject Him in eternity, He will never reject them. Far from finding the word *inclusion* to be perilous, you will see it as a precious word. You will recognize God as the one who has included us all from the beginning. He is the God who has successfully brought us into union with Himself and now, by His Spirit, seeks to reveal the reality to us that already existed even before we knew or believed it. He is the God whose accomplishment in the incarnation is, to quote the Apostle Paul, "much more" than anything Adam ever did to humanity. He is the God who is indeed filled to overflowing with hyper-grace just like His hyper-love toward those who were trapped in hyper-sin. Now, having come to know Him, they have only one thing to say to God—*"Hyper thank you!"*

## Did God Exclude Some?

If you hear somebody condemn the idea of inclusion, ask them this question: "Who is excluded from God's love as expressed in Jesus Christ?" Who are the people that God doesn't love? Who are the ones for whom Jesus did not die? How could the announcement of the Christmas angel be "good news of great joy which will be for all the people" if not everybody was included? How did Jesus "taste death for every man" if He didn't actually deal with every single person's sin? Either God is love and has committed Himself to a relationship to humanity or he is not the god Jesus came to reveal.

The Bible isn't vague about the matter when it says, "For as in Adam all die, even so in Christ all shall be made alive" (1 Corinthians 5:22). This verse isn't talking about one "all" in the first part of the verse and another "all" in the last part. All is all.

Who is included in Christ? Consider this verse in Colossians 3:11: "Words like Jewish and non-Jewish, religious and irreligious, insider and outsider, uncivilized and uncouth, slave and free, mean nothing. From now on everyone is defined by Christ, everyone is included in Christ" (*The Message*).

If you enjoy digging deeper into the Scripture, grab your resource materials and dig in to a study of Romans 5:11. "And not only this, but we also exult in God through our Lord Jesus Christ, through whom we have now received the reconciliation." This one verse can transform your perspective about whether it is our decision for Him that causes us to be included or His decision for us.

The word reconciled has rich meaning in this verse. The original language of the New Testament uses a Greek word (translated "reconcile") that literally means "to exchange." The connotation of the word pointed toward money changers who would take your foreign national currency and exchange it for the money used in the country where you were.

What Paul is saying here is that our life in Adam has been exchanged for another life. Adam's life has been taken away from us and we have been given Christ's life in its place. We don't have Adamic life anymore. When Jesus died, Adam's race died with Him. Just like all humanity had been in Adam when he committed his act of disobedience, so were we all in Jesus when He committed his act of obedience. Just like everybody experienced the consequences of Adam's deed so did we all experience the consequences of Jesus's deed.

Romans 5:19 explains: "For as through the one man's disobedience the many were made sinners, even so through the obedience of the One the many will be made righteous." The cause and effect with both Adam and Jesus are clear. Adam's disobedience caused the many to become sinners and Jesus's obedience caused the many to be righteous. In both instances, somebody did something and everybody was affected as the result. It wasn't what we did that was the cause. It was what they did that impacted us.

Don't get confused about the phrase "the many" by thinking it doesn't mean everybody. All is many. We all were included in what Jesus did just as we all were included in what Adam did. To believe otherwise is to place the power of Adam's disobedience above the obedience of Jesus.

When the word "reconciled" is used here, it is in what is called "the passive voice" in the Greek language in which the New Testament was written. Simply put, that means those about whom the word speaks were not active in the process. They did nothing. They were passive while the thing happened.

In this case, the verse shows that we had nothing to do with our reconciliation. This exchanged life we now have isn't because we did something. We were passive in the process. God made it happen and we simply benefit from what He did. We are the objects of this reconciliation and the subject is God. We didn't reconcile ourselves to Him by our decision. He reconciled us to Himself by His eternal decision that was made before the foundation of the world. "It is by His doing that we are in Christ Jesus" (1 Corinthians 1:30) and "not of ourselves" (see Ephesians 2:8). This reconciliation was a gift from God.

In Jesus Christ, our disobedience was exchanged for obedience; our rebellion was exchanged for submission; our faithlessness was exchanged for faithfulness; and our death in Adam was exchanged for a new life in Christ. What Jesus did rescued everybody who was trapped in Adam from sin's consequence, and in its place gave us the benefits of being a child of God—one who has been adopted in Jesus Christ. No wonder Paul wrote that we exult (rejoice, are very happy, glory) in God through our Lord Jesus Christ!

God's purposes are not held captive by the frail human will of people about whom the Apostle Paul wrote, "There is no one who seeks God" (Romans 3:11). Thankfully, it didn't depend on us. "For the Son of Man came to seek and to save those who are lost" (Luke 19:10) and, to His glory and our good, He succeeded.

Paul wrote in another place about whether or not God's mercy is shown only to those who decided to trust Him. In Romans 9:15-16 he wrote, "For He says to Moses, 'I will have mercy on whom I have mercy, and I will have compassion on whom I have compassion.' So then it does not depend on the man who wills or the man who runs, but on God who has mercy."

## What About Free Will?

Does the mercy of God depend on human will? Consider the meaning of the word *will*. It comes from the Greek word *thelo* and it means, "to be resolved or determined, to purpose, to desire, to wish." Look at that definition. Now compare it with what you have been told about how one experiences God's mercy.

The predominant message of the modern church world is that God will show people mercy *if they want it*. If they choose, exercising their will, to *let* Him have His way with them, He will show them His mercy by reconciling, justifying, forgiving and giving them His life. So the message of the legalistic church world is that God wants to do something for you but you must *decide* to let Him do it. It is up to the will of the person as to whether or not God will be merciful to them.

Now, go back and look at these verses again. What does the Bible say here? God said that He would have mercy on whom *He* would have mercy and have compassion on whom *He* would have compassion. Where does human will come into that equation? What does verse sixteen say in response to that question?

Thank God, His mercy does not depend on our will but on His will. It isn't our commitment to Him that causes Him to be merciful and compassionate to us. It is His commitment to us! The doctrine of the cross has been subtly replaced with a doctrine of commitment that suggests we are the ones who have the authority to decide whether the incarnation was a waste or not. Well, it wasn't, and that decision is not in question anyway.

God didn't wait for us to seek Him. He came to seek us and we have been found. He didn't come to rescue only a few of us but to reconcile everybody in Adam's race back to His Father. This isn't to say that everybody has believed the gospel and knows Jesus but it does mean that the gospel is true whether we believe it or not and *God knows us!*

The Bible reveals the subject of salvation through two lenses: the lens of universality and the lens of particularity. The universal aspect of the gospel doesn't mean that everybody is a Christian or that everybody goes to heaven. Instead, it speaks of the scope of what Christ has done and its efficacy on those affected. It does not speak to the particular response of people toward what He has done.

The modern church has stressed *particularity* to the exclusion of the teaching of the Bible about the *universality* of the work of Christ. Of course, people must believe the gospel. That is particularity. However, their unbelief doesn't negate the reality of what Jesus has done for all people. That is universality.

The gospel is the universally good news of what He has done for every person. Consider each of these verses and determine who is included in what they say:

❖ John 3:16 For God so loved the world that He gave His only begotten Son.

❖ 1 John 4:9 This is how God showed His love among us: He sent His one and only Son into the world that we might live through Him.

❖ 1 John 4:14 And we have seen and testify that the Father has sent His Son to be the Savior of the world.

❖ 2 Corinthians 5:19 God was in Christ reconciling the world to Himself.

Are these verses of universality or particularity? Who is included in what they say? The witness of Scripture is that our Father is a God of Inclusion. In Jesus Christ, He has embraced us all and now simply calls on us to repent by changing our minds about who He is and receive Him too.

# CHAPTER FOUR
## The Anchor of Identity

For the past week I have spent each evening watching DVD episodes of an old television mini-series called *Roots*, a filmed adaptation of the Alex Haley novel. The story chronicles the hundred-year saga of Africans captured and brought to America by slave traders. One scene in an episode I watched recently particularly struck me with its spiritual implications.

In the scene the new *massa* (master) had renamed one of the "young bucks" he had purchased at auction. The slave's real name was Kunta Kinte but the slave owner renamed him as Toby. The problem was that Kunta had refused to accept his new name and wouldn't respond to it when called by that name. His insistence on clinging to his original name had given him a sense of empowerment about his true identity and had instilled in him the courage to take a chance by trying to escape.

In this episode he had been caught after having run away. He had been brought back to the plantation and was tied to a post where he was receiving lashes from a bull whip.

"What is your name?" the master asked him.

"Kunta," he replied. "Kunta Kinte."

Another fierce lash cut his back.

"What is your name?" the master again shouted.

"Kunta Kinte!" the slave cried.

Another brutal strike cut across his body.

"What is your name?" the angry master screamed.

"Kunta," he replied again and again.

After what seemed like an eternity of brutality, one final lash left Kunta in such agony that he was barely able to speak.

"What is your name?" the master asked.

"Toby," he finally answered. "My name is Toby."

"That's right," replied the plantation owner. "Your name is Toby."

As I watched that scene, I thought about how true the reality represented by it is for all of us. Every one of us has been given an original identity by our Creator. We are made in His image. The Bible explains it saying that we were "created in righteousness and holiness" (Ephesians 4:24). We all have a shared heritage that finds its roots in Him. "Do we not all have one Father?" one prophet asked. (See Malachi 2:10.)

When God looked at the humans that He had created, He said, "It is good." Our original identity was based on the union we have with

Him. Living in the recognition of that union, mankind was suited for anything this world would call upon him to do. He didn't live by his own self-sufficiency but experienced life as an expression of his relationship to God.

Sin coming into the world changed all that. When Adam ate from the Tree of the Knowledge of Good and Evil, darkness descended upon mankind. Like Kunta Kinte, Adam was captured and carried away by a cruel master and found himself living in a land where he had never been—a world of sin. In that place he forgot his identity because He lost the conscious connection to his God—his True Home.

Humanity's plight was also described in another dramatic story. In *The Lord of the Rings,* when Sméagol, who had become known as Gollum, spoke of his own oppressors, he described the tragedy of it: "They cursed us. Murderer they called us. They cursed us, and drove us away. And we wept. Precious, we wept to be so alone. And we only wish to catch fish so juicy sweet. And we forgot the taste of bread... the sound of the trees... the softness of the wind. We even forgot our own name."

Once one has forgotten his own name, the only hope he has is that a miracle will happen. Otherwise, his lifestyle will morph into one that matches the false identity that has been imposed upon him. He needs a deliverer.

Jesus is that Deliverer. The coming of Jesus Christ into this world was a rescue mission. Our Triune God refused to leave us in such a sad and helpless state of affairs. We were lost and could not find our way through the darkness and back to our resting place in Him, so He came to bring us there. What we could not do, He did for us.

As the Last Adam, Jesus solved the problem brought upon mankind by the first Adam by undoing what he had done. Adam's race died with Jesus Christ, was buried with Him and now has been raised to walk in new life—*His* life. When you want to learn your roots, if you stop with Adam you aren't going back far enough to see your true place of origin. Our roots are in Jesus Christ who created us. (See Colossians 1:16.)

## Being a Child Of God

When the Apostle Paul spoke to the pagans on Mars Hill, he talked to them about the matter of their identity. These Athenians had forgotten their own name and, like people everywhere who don't know the truth, they were scrambling in a frantic search to establish an identity. They had built more idols than you could count, just to cover all the bases, but Paul spoke to them about the "unknown God" that they needed to know.

In Acts 17, the Bible recounts how he told them of the true God who had created all mankind from one man; the God who had drawn the boundaries between the nations of the world; the God who had put in them the very hunger for Him that they were trying to satisfy in all the wrong ways by worshipping false Gods.

Then he brought these unbelieving pagans to the focal point of the whole matter when he told them, "Even some of your own poets have said, 'For we also are His children'" (Acts 17:28). With those words, Paul brought them face-to-face with the truth about their identity. "We also are His children," he said to them.

Were these unbelieving pagans really children of God? Read Acts 17:28 and see for yourself what the man who wrote two thirds of the New Testament and who arguably understood more about God's grace than anybody before him told them. Yes, they were God's children. That's what Paul said.

Had they professed faith in Jesus Christ? No, they didn't even know the gospel until Paul preached it to them. Yet, He still told them that they were children of God. How was that possible? Don't people become children of God by believing in Him? Here's how the Bible answers in Ephesians 1:3-6:

*Blessed be the God and Father of our Lord Jesus Christ, who has blessed*

*us with every spiritual blessing in the heavenly places in Christ, just as he*

*chose us in Him before the foundation of the world, that we would be holy*

*and blameless before Him. In love he predestined us to adoption through*

*Jesus Christ to Himself, according to the kind intention of His will, to the praise*

*of the glory of His grace, which He freely bestowed on us in the Beloved.*

How does one become a child of God? It was through our adoption in Jesus Christ before time began. Without so much as a nod of approval on our part, but purely "according to the kind intention of His will," our God chose us "in (Jesus Christ) before the foundation of the world." Make no mistake about it—this was a done deal from the beginning. You aren't a child of God because *you* did something. What child can boast about how she got herself born? No, the child has nothing to do with that.

When one believes in Jesus Christ, one simply moves into the experiential awareness of the reality that had already existed. It reminds me of my dear friend Paul Anderson-Walsh from England. Paul is a black man but isn't as dark-skinned as many. He lived in an orphanage as a child.

Paul tells the story of the time when, as an adolescent, he was placed in an orphanage where all the children were black. He went to the nun in charge and said, "Sister, I don't think I can stay here."

"Why not, Paul?" she asked.

"Well," he said, "I'm not sure I can live with all these black people."

"Sit down, Paul," the nun advised. "We need to talk."

It's humorous now to think that Paul didn't even know he was black until he was told. Once he understood that he was black, he found himself gravitating toward the black culture of his youth. He began to enjoy the music of black singers and the movies of black actors. He even grew an Afro hairdo. Having been notified of his identity, his lifestyle began to conform to the truth with no struggle on his part. The truth had set him free to become who he already was.

When people understand and believe the truth about their identity, conversion takes place. It's inevitable. That's why the Apostle Paul made identity the core of the message he told the unbelievers on Mars Hill. Having told them the truth about who they were, he then drew the evangelistic net: "Being then the children of God, we ought not to think that the Divine Nature is like gold or silver or stone, an image formed by the art and thought of man" (Acts 17:29).

Notice how he called on these unbelievers to see the truth about who they were and about how it contrasted with the lifestyle they were living. Then he strikes the gospel appeal: "Therefore having overlooked the times of ignorance, God is now declaring to men that all people everywhere should repent" (17:30).

He told them the truth about who they were—children of God. Then he called on them to repent, to change their minds and believe in Christ. *That* is what a proper presentation of the gospel looks like. We proclaim the good news to people and then challenge them to repent (change their minds), believe and receive it.

What happened? The same thing that happens today. Some made fun of him. Others said they'd think about it. "But some men joined him and believed" (17:34).

What is this identity message I'm discussing? What are its traits? If this is an anchor for life that needs to be central to us, it is important to understand what we mean when we talk about our identity in Christ.

## We Live In Union With God

The most important thing to understand about our identity in Christ revolves around the relationship we have to God through Him. Because we are in Christ, there is no separation between Him and ourselves. The Bible teaches that the person who is joined together to Him is one spirit with Him. (See 1 Corinthians 6:17.) Jesus Christ isn't simply *in* our lives. The news is much better than that. We are actually one with Him. There is no distance between us. As Paul told the pagans to whom he preached, "In Him we live and move and exist."

Separation from God is only an illusion. It doesn't exist. The only alienation between man and God is in our minds. The Apostle Paul told the Colossians that they were once "alienated in your minds" but that's the extent of it. (See Colossians 1:21.) In Jesus Christ there is no distance. Ephesians 2:13 says, "But now you have been united with Christ Jesus. Once you were far away from God, but now you have been brought near to Him through the blood of Christ." Everybody for whom Jesus shed His blood has been brought into union with God and, as we discussed in an earlier chapter, He shed His blood for all.

Through the years, to illustrate our union with God, I've used the illustration of how southerners in the United States make sweet tea. Unlike other parts of the country, we don't stir sugar into iced tea after it has been served. When we boil the tea bags in the pan of water on the stove, we add the sugar immediately after taking the scalding concentrate off the burner and before putting it into the pitcher. That way the sugar dissolves and becomes inseparably joined to the tea. The two have become one.

Put sugar in a glass of iced tea and stir it all you want but, when you finish stirring, the sugar will begin to settle in the bottom of the glass. You have sugar in the glass of tea but the two are still separate. Boil the tea bags in water and then add the sugar immediately, and there aren't two separate ingredients anymore. They are now in union.

Jesus isn't in our lives like sugar in the glass of iced tea. Jesus *is* your life because you have become "a partaker of the divine nature" (2 Peter 1:4). In Jesus Christ, we have been joined into union with our Triune God in such a way that there is no life apart from Him. He *is* our life and we live each moment in this amazing union.

Just as Paul saw people who were in union with God when he spoke to the unbelievers on Mars Hill (Acts 17), we are to understand that in Christ our God has reconciled the world to Himself. (See 2 Corinthians 5:19.) The core of the message of identity is the union we all now have with our God through Jesus Christ.

## *We Are Holy*

To be holy is often associated with a squeaky-clean lifestyle but that understanding isn't what the Bible means when it uses the word. Even inanimate objects are called holy in Scripture. The temple in the Old Testament was called the "holy temple." God called the ground where Moses stood before the burning bush "holy ground." The utensils the priests used were called holy. So it is obvious then that the word can't refer to behavior, since objects have no ability to behave in any way.

The word actually means "to be set apart." The temple, the utensils that the priests used, and even the ground where Moses stood were set apart for a particular divine purpose. The same is true with people. God has chosen us for the specific purpose of sharing in His life with us.

Does this affect the way we live our lives? Absolutely! When we understand that we are holy because He has chosen to give us His life and then live His life through us in this world, which becomes a huge catalyst for living a holy lifestyle. We don't focus on trying to live religiously or even morally. Instead, we focus on Christ and, as we do, we will discover that His life effortlessly flows out of us. The way Jesus described it was like "a river flowing from your innermost being" (See John 7:38). We don't have to pump it out by self-effort. His life flows out of us like a mighty current of water that rushes out, drenching our environment with His presence.

When Peter went to the house of Cornelius, he made a statement to those unbelieving Gentiles that was shocking to the religious world of his day. He said, "God has shown me that I should not call any man unholy or unclean" (Acts 10:28). What a revelation! Aren't only believers holy? This mindset of exclusion is the same one Peter had when he thought that only Jews were holy and that Gentiles couldn't possibly be. That's why God told Peter not to call any man *unclean*. That word refers to the kosher status—the Jewish standard for cleanness.

God caused Peter to know that it wasn't just Jews who are "kosher." We all are.

Many Christians today have the same mindset about unbelievers that Peter had about Gentiles. They think unbelievers couldn't possibly be holy. After all, they haven't believed! But God also told Peter not to call any man *unholy*. If that was true for Peter, it is also true for us two millennia later.

What causes a person to be holy? Is it belief in Christ? Do we make ourselves holy by doing that? Not according to the Bible. 1 Corinthians 1:30 says, "It is *because of him* that you are in Christ Jesus, who has become for us wisdom from God—that is, our righteousness, *holiness*, and redemption" (*NIV*, emphasis added). Look at the verse and answer this: A person is holy because of—*who*? Is it our own action in believing that makes it true? No, the Bible plainly says it is "because of Him." We are holy because He set us apart for Himself and not because of something we have done—even believing. *He* is our source of holiness, not our belief.

## We Are a Masterpiece

Perhaps the greatest plague on contemporary culture is the prevailing sense of insecurity that people feel about themselves. Bombarded with media advertising and programming that present people who seem to have it all together in every way, it's hard not to feel inferior. They have perfect bodies and beautiful mates and fantastic jobs and well behaved children and lots of money and... Well, you get the picture. If you buy into it, it's enough to depress you.

The facts of the real world are that life is hard at times. If we determine our value based on what circumstances would have us believe, very few of us would judge ourselves as being people of great value. Life experiences usually tell most of us otherwise.

That's why we can't determine our value based on the verdict of circumstances or even other people. The only one who can accurately assess our value is the one who created us. He alone knows what we are worth and His appraisal of us is correct.

Imagine finding a huge diamond ring on the ground. The first question that would come to your mind would be, "I wonder if it's a *real* diamond?" You would probably first excitedly show it to friends and family. Each of them would have an opinion about the matter. One might tell you, "That looks exactly like a diamond ring somebody I know owns! It *is* real. I know it is!" Somebody else might say, "No, I've seen this before. It's cubic zirconia. It's pretty but not worth very much."

Everybody you showed it to would have an opinion. There's only one way you could find the true value. That would be to take the ring to a jeweler who could do a legitimate appraisal. His appraisal of the ring's value would be determined by its authenticity and on what price the ring would bring on the open market. What somebody else would pay for it would be its value.

Now, think about the value of a human being. What are we actually worth? If you ask other people, there will be a diversity of answers. Somebody's supervisor at work probably won't have the same opinion as the person's mother would have. There's really only one way to know our value and that is to get an appraisal from The Expert.

The One who created humans would know because not only did He make us but He also bought us. The Bible says, "you have been bought with a price" (see 1 Corinthians 6:20), and the One who bought you knows your worth. What was the price that God paid for us? It was His own Son. The price He was willing to pay was Himself. He gave His life for you to ensure that you would always be His possession.

If the ring would sell for ten thousand dollars, would it be accurate to say that the value of the ring equals that amount of money? Of course it would. In the same way, our God gave Himself for every person He created. The staggering implication of that fact is that our value to our Father is equal to the value of His own Son. That *is* what He paid for us.

Ephesians 2:10 says, "You are His workmanship created in Christ Jesus." The word *workmanship* in the verse is the Greek word *poema,* from which we derive the word *poem.* Make no mistake about it: each of us is a divine work of art who has been carefully and lovingly crafted by God. With divine inspiration arising from a heart filled with love, He has brought us into existence for His own pleasure.

Our joy as believers is to share the wonderful gospel with others, telling them that God loves them and that they are a treasure to Him. This is the beginning of evangelism based on grace. We don't come at people with threats but with love. The gospel is good news and it isn't possible to angrily tell good news!

The anchor of inclusion is paramount if we are to embrace and express God's grace to people. Knowing who you are is necessary to lead others to understanding their own identity. An identity crisis has plagued the world. People's minds have been stolen away from the truth of their home in the trinitarian circle of the Godhead. I end this chapter by asking you, "What is *your* name?" That's right—you are a child of God who, living in union with Him, is a holy masterpiece.

# CHAPTER FIVE
## The Anchor of Practical Grace

Grace is nothing more than another doctrine if the only value it brings us is increased head knowledge. Wisdom is the ability to apply knowledge to life. The presence of God's grace in our lives isn't there simply for our gratification, although there's certainly nothing wrong with feeling gratified by the experience of Divine Love within us. How else could we possibly feel? However, it's not just about that because the effect of grace in our lives reaches out to every part of our lifestyle.

Grace changes how we see God, causing us to understand Him to be a relational, loving, inclusive God who has bestowed His very nature upon us and given us an identity defined by His life and love for us. It is impossible to truly understand that without experiencing the flow of His life and love into every corner and crevice of our lives in this world.

Understanding the truth about who He is and who we are changes everything. It gives us a new attitude and leads to actions that express the Truth we possess. Grace isn't simply a topic to be studied. It is a dynamic, life-giving Force that permeates our being like salt permeates the oceans of the world, like oxygen saturates the air you are breathing right now. God's grace flows out of us and changes our environment for the simple reason that the presence of Jesus *always* changes the environment.

Grace is practical in that it makes a huge difference in the way we think and feel and act. If these three areas of our lives haven't been transformed by grace, then we need to continue to pray, study and open ourselves to seeing the Spirit of Grace reveal Himself to us in a greater way because you can be sure—grace transforms. It is practical in every part of our lives.

### Grace Defines Your Inner Self

At its most basic level, the grace of God will inwardly change people in ways that are deep and personal. Grace is more than theological. It is anthropological. That is to say, it is the means by which God embraces man. In others words, it's not just a biblical way of describing Him—not just a theological proposition—but it is a *power* that rebuilds our lives so that how we live conforms to the reality of what He has already accomplished in our spirits. Simply put, grace changes people inwardly by the power of His indwelling life.

Looking into your own life experience, how does His grace affect you in the practical ways you think about yourself? Here are a few questions that might help you see the extent to which you have been transformed by grace.

- ❖ Do you live free from self-condemnation and feelings of inferiority?

- ❖ Do you know that your sins have been removed and you are now guilt-free?

- ❖ Do you know that God adores you just like you are, at this very moment?

- ❖ Are you free from the struggle to improve yourself by doing religious things?

- ❖ Are you confident about your eternal home with Him?

- ❖ Is your focus on Him and not on yourself and how well you are or aren't acting?

❖ Are you trusting in His control over your life in every situation?

❖ Are you at peace about both your past and your future?

These questions aren't intended to cause you to feel like you're failing if your answers aren't what you want them to be. None of us can give the perfect answer to all of these questions because we are all still in process. Your answers do help to reveal, however, the extent to which you may still need to lean in on Him in prayer and faith. He will cause you to experience the healing and transformation you may need in those areas of your personal life.

The bottom line is that *grace makes an internal difference* when we understand it. How do we grow in these areas of our personal lives? We do it by focusing on Him. When we do that, we will experience what the Bible calls "the renewal of your mind."

Don't beat yourself up if you don't see yourself as being very far along in this journey. This practical aspect of apply grace to your inner life can be a challenge if you have been indoctrinated by religious paradigms that suggest that it is up to you to make things happen spiritually in your life. Make no mistake about it—you cannot grow yourself spiritually. Only He can cause you to grow and He will. Put your eyes on Him and when you sense His Spirit showing you ways that you need to change your mind about yourself, do it! Don't allow past indoctrination to cause you to dispute what your Creator says about you. Repent (change your mind) and confess (agree with Him) about who He is, who you are and about your relationship with one another.

You will be anchored for every storm of life when you apply the practicality of grace to your inner self and see yourself for who you really are, and not for the person you may sometimes feel like or even act like. Let Him define you. By His power, change the way you think and your actions will follow.

## *Grace Will Influence Your Family*

After grace reshapes our inner selves so that we begin to experience internal freedom and peace, the next step is that it begins to flow outward into the relationships we have with others. That starts at home. Grace never shines brighter than when it is on display in our families.

Surely there is no place where the practicality of grace is more helpful than in the relationship between a husband and wife. The greatest object lesson in this world that illustrates humanity's union with God is marriage. Nothing reveals more clearly the relational aspect of the Father, Son and Spirit than the marriage relationship. The Apostle Paul affirmed this when he wrote, "Therefore a man shall leave his father and mother and hold fast to his wife and the two shall become one flesh. This mystery is profound, and I am saying that it refers to Christ and the church" (Ephesians 5:31-32).

What does a marriage governed by grace look like? It looks like the relationship He has with us. In fact, it looks like the relationship among the members of the Godhead. As we experience Him as the source of our relationship, there will be aspects of our marriage that are clearly the manifestation of His life in it.

## Sacrificial Love

The Bible says that "Christ loved the church and gave Himself for her" (Ephesians 5:25). This statement immediately follows Paul's admonition to men to love their wives. What does it mean to give oneself for another? Some have diluted the power of this verse by suggesting that they love their spouse enough that, like Jesus, they would die for the one they love.

The fact is that to die for your mate would likely be easier than what the core meaning of the verse actually teaches. Christ didn't just die for us. He *lived* for us, too. His life in this world was a vicarious life on our behalf. His life was your life before the Father. He did nothing that wasn't motivated by His desire and intention to raise you up so that you could live seated squarely in the circle of the Father, Son and Spirit. His obedience, baptism, faithfulness, everything—it was for your benefit.

Grace will empower us in the same way in our marriages. When the life of Jesus permeates our thoughts and attitude toward our spouse, we will lay aside any self-centered desires we may have, and we will live our lives in a way that is motivated by what is best for the one we love. Trinitarian life is others-centered love and there is nowhere that becomes more apparent than in marriage.

As grace increasingly leads you in your marriage, you will find yourself laying aside your rights for the good of your spouse. The Bible says about Jesus, "He gave up his divine privileges; he took the humble position of a slave and was born as a human being" (Philippians 2:7). Jesus came into this world with all the rights and prerogatives of being God but He *chose* to empty Himself of those rights. He became a man and *as a man* showed us what it looks like when somebody puts the one he loves above himself.

Giving up divine privilege wasn't something Jesus did just one time. It was something He did every day. Can you imagine how many times He could have taken over and forced His will on those around Him? He *knew* His way would always be the best way in every situation. How many times might He have imposed His knowledge, His ability, and His human desires on those He loved. But He didn't. Time after time, He chose to stand down and lovingly yield to what He knew were less than perfect situations because of His love for others. Even when He was "oppressed and treated harshly, He never said a word." (See

Isaiah 53:7, *NLT*.) What a picture—the God who created us surrendering His rights even when we were wrong.

This is where grace becomes most practical. We all want to have things our way but grace miraculously empowers us to surrender our rights to the desires of the person we love. It teaches us that we win by realizing we don't have to win.

Arguments in marriage always arise when two people are each insisting that their rights and their perspective must prevail. "But I am *right* about this!" our thoughts scream within us in those heated moments. What would happen in a marriage where both people gave up those rights, and we were willing to yield to our partner? "But things would sometimes turn out horribly!" might be the response. Yes, that's true. In fact, one time when One Person laid down His right to be right, it led to Him being crucified. Apparently even knowing that sacrificing our rights may lead to a painful outcome, it is *still* the best way to express love.

The Bible says, "Do nothing from selfishness or empty conceit, but with humility of mind regard one another as more important than yourselves" (Philippians 2:3). What would happen in life if we all took that approach with our mates? Selfless, sacrificial surrendering of personal entitlement—what will *that* look like as it grows in your marriage?

## Building Up Each Other

Grace is always constructive and is never destructive. The GPS in all our relationships is determined by the answer to this question: "What is the most loving thing I can do right now toward this person?" Grace will empower you to let this guiding principle of Christ's life direct you in the relationship you have to your family.

Children need gracious guidance. Sometimes grace requires a gentle embrace. At other times it calls for stern correction. At all times it equips us to act in the most constructive way toward our mate and our children. This is the practicality of grace at home. It is the way Jesus lives His life through us in the privacy of our family.

Children don't require perfection from their parents but what they do want is authenticity. It isn't mere religious instruction that will teach them Christ. It is the recognition that Jesus is the thread that creates the fabric of their family. "In Him we live and move and exist" at home just like in every other place we find ourselves in this world. Children need to understand that our relationship to Christ doesn't revolve around the things we do, but is grounded in personal intimacy with Him.

Is there a place for discipline in a home governed by grace? Are there rules to be established and enforced? Yes, these too are practical expressions of grace at home.

Rules aren't legalistic across the board. Legalism is the system of living in which we try to make spiritual progress or gain God's blessings based on what we do. It has to do with our relationship to God.

To make a rule that your child go to her room to pray and read her Bible every day is legalistic. To set a rule about cleaning her room is not legalistic. If you want her to learn to pray and read her Bible, model that for her. Do it with her. That builds up your child. To be assigned time to go to her room and read the Bible the way a child would be given the task of brushing her teeth before bedtime is not constructive.

What about the rule concerning cleaning her room? Isn't that legalistic, too? No, because *legalism has to do with our walk with God*. Rules are not inherently wrong. Children must learn that there are responsibilities that we each must assume in order for life to flow smoothly.

Set loving rules of the house for your children and see that they are followed. This builds up a child, teaching him to act responsibly in small matters so that he will know how to act responsibly in large matters later in life. This is where grace at home becomes practical.

Rules should always be so embedded in love that the children don't see them as being in contrast to love. Discipline for misbehavior builds up a child when it is carried out in a way that communicates love and not anger. If you have children, you need no explanation here about why grace flowing through your own life is necessary for this to happen! It is important to *respond, not react,* to misbehavior. Despite how it often feels to parents in the heat of the moment, Jesus can actually empower you to do that.

The practicality of grace anchors us at home by guiding us in how to express the life of Jesus in the most important place of our lives—with our family. Love your spouse and your children. Lift them so that they become more Christlike in their lifestyles as they respond to you allowing Him to express His life through your lifestyle at home.

## Bringing Christ to Culture

As the circle of Christ widens through our lifestyles, we then move beyond our families and bring Him into the surrounding culture. Jesus said, "Let your light shine before men in such a way that they may see your good works, and glorify your Father who is in heaven" (Matthew 5:16). Do you see the practicality of grace in the way it first profoundly impacts us in a personal way, then spills over into our families and ultimately infiltrates our culture through us?

Our lives in this world are an expression of Him. As we trust Him to live through us, we are light in a dark world. Here is where the importance of the practicality of grace becomes clear. *We are to be agents of change in our culture.*

Legalism grows in a climate of exclusion and isolationism. It is the mindset that causes a believer to withdraw from society, seeing it as an evil environment to be avoided lest we become contaminated by it. It is a fear-based mentality that fails to recognize the fact that "the Spirit who lives in you is greater than the spirit who lives in the world" (1 John 4:4, *NLT*), and we have nothing to fear.

A person trapped in legalism sets himself as an opponent to the culture around him. He is proud of the fact that he isn't "worldly" but is separated from society. I've seen legalists actually take pride in their ignorance of culture. This is not the way of grace. A proper understanding of Scripture leads to the realization that we are to be Christ's ambassadors to culture, not holy hermits gone into hiding. (See 2 Corinthians 5:20.) Legalists come out of hiding only long enough to shout at the world. They believe the only reason for associating with the culture at large is to correct and convert it. Sadly, the very thing they want to do could be accomplished if they could only learn to love it. When the Bible tells them to not love the world, they have mistakenly come to think it means they must avoid it lest their acceptance of people there imply that they love a sinful world system.

They think that when the Bible says we are to be "in the world but not of the world" that it means we are to withdraw. However, to retreat from the culture around us isn't what the Bible teaches. A person who is afraid that she may become soiled by being in a sinful environment hasn't come to see herself for the light and salt that she is. A sinful environment doesn't change the person walking in grace. *We change our environment.*

Jesus was a friend of sinners. Some believers try to distance themselves from anybody they deem to be a sinner. There was a group in Jesus's day who did that too. They were called *Pharisees.* The word means, "separated ones." Read the New Testament and you'll find that Jesus didn't have kind words to say about that group.

Grace shows up in practical ways when we relax and learn to live our lives in the confidence that the Christ who indwells us will reveal Himself to others through us. A person walking in grace is a thermostat for our culture, not a thermometer in it. We don't adjust ourselves to the climate around us. We reset the temperature by allowing the love of Christ to flow out of us through our words and actions.

Those who live in grace aren't passive about cultural problems. We recognize the need to share the gospel with individuals so that they might know Jesus Christ, but we also don't dismiss the social implications of the gospel. Legalists decry "the social gospel" and rightly so, if it leaves out the need for personal faith in Christ. On the other hand, many have wrongly thought that the gospel has no news for the social needs of culture. That, too, is a mistake. Our gospel is intended to impact humanity both individually and collectively. Those who walk in grace are to work together to make a difference in this world at both the individual level and the societal level.

## Grace Really Is Practical

On one occasion when Paul was preaching in Thessalonica, there was an uproar about his message. Opponents of the gospel dragged some of the believers out of their homes and brought them before city officials. "These men who have turned the world upside down have come here too," they said. (See Acts, 17:6, *Holman Christian Standard Bible.*)

Can you imagine having such an impact on a city that it would cause this kind of charge to be brought against you? That's what grace can do. It can turn the world upside down. The practical possibilities of the impact that grace can have on our culture are limitless. Let's carry this wonderful gospel of grace from the church to the culture and turn our world upside down or, from the true perspective—right-side up.

# CONCLUSION
## Anchoring Together

There is a lot of wind blowing across the waters of the church world today. There are gentle south winds that soothe the soul with the message of grace. There are strong nor'easters that trouble people with thunderous proclamations of a god who is angry and punitive. There's no small amount of hot air that comes from pulpits in an effort to pump people up to carry out the legalistic demands that their sectarian group believes are necessary to live the Christian life.

With so many winds coming from so many directions, it is imperative that we all hold onto the anchors discussed in this book. These five truths are the core of what it means to embrace grace and to live in it each day. There is really only one wind you need. The word for that wind in the original language of the New Testament is *pneuma*. It's the word from which the English word *pneumonia* is derived. We also use the word when we speak of a *pneumatic* tool, one that is powered by air. As you can tell, the word has to do with air—with wind.

When the word is used in the New Testament, it is translated as *spirit*. The Spirit of Christ is called the Holy *pneuma*. Jesus made the connection between the Spirit and the wind when He said, "The wind blows where it wishes and you hear the sound of it, but do not know where it comes from and where it is going: so is everyone who is born of the Spirit" (John 3:8).

Some of the best memories in my life have been times when I have slept below deck on a sailboat. The gentle rocking of the boat, the sound of the wind lightly blowing through the rigging, and the soft slapping of waves against the hull create a euphoric environment that lends itself to a great night's sleep. It's hard to find a pleasure to compare to a night like that in paradise. When the anchor is set firmly there is no reason for any concern. It's possible to simply enjoy the experience with complete contentment.

The five anchoring truths of this book can enable you to experience life with a serenity and joy that you may have never known until now. Embrace these truths and allow them to saturate your whole perspective on life. Watch how being anchored satisfies the spiritual desires you have sensed in the past. Grow in grace and in your knowledge of Jesus Christ as you understand more and more about His love for all mankind.

I wrote this book as the result of a teaching I shared with our Grace Walk team at our International Leadership Summit in 2014. At that meeting, I discussed the doctrinal framework one needs to accept to be a formal part of our organization. If what you've read in this book resonates in your spirit as truth and you want to connect with others, there are ways to do that.

If you would like to connect with others who believe this message and celebrate it together in informal small groups, you can find those people by going to www.gracewalk.org/groups. There you will find Grace Walk Groups who regularly meet together to encourage one another in our journey in grace. If you are interested in starting a group with like-minded people in your area, the site will give you information about how to do that.

I would be happy if you are interested in formally becoming a part of our Grace Walk team. Right now Grace Walk has offices in seven countries and groups in many places around the world. If you want to belong to an organization that will encourage you and where you can be an encouragement to others, please let us know through the link I've provided for the Grace Walk Groups.

You can also grow in the message of grace through books, audio and video resources available in my online store at www.gracewalkresources.com. If you want a more complete and expanded study of the things discussed in this book, you will enjoy my book *Beyond An Angry God*. The book can be purchased in the online store I've referenced in this paragraph, as well as other online and local bookstores.

Finally, I invite you to visit www.beyondanangrygod.com to watch videos and read articles about the subject matter of this book. There is much available there for you at no cost that I know will be of help.

If you have been encouraged by reading *Anchored in Life,* I would be glad to hear from you. You can email me at:

stevemcvey@gracewalk.org

Or write to:

> Dr. Steve McVey
> Grace Walk
> P.O. Box 6537
> Douglasville, Georgia 30135

Thank you for taking the time to read *Anchored in Life* and may you be richly blessed as you move forward in your own grace walk!

# ABOUT THE AUTHOR

Dr. Steve McVey is the founder of Grace Walk Ministries, with his home office in Atlanta, Georgia and satellite offices in six other countries. He is the author of eighteen books including the bestselling *Grace Walk*. More than 550,000 copies of his books have been translated into fourteen languages. McVey's focus is on the grace of God and how to live in the freedom of walking in grace.

## WHAT OTHERS HAVE SAID ABOUT STEVE McVEY'S BOOKS

❖ Grammy Award-winning gospel singer Kirk Franklin said, "Steve McVey's books have been used by God to transform my Christian walk."

❖ Dr. Tony Evans, President of The Urban Alternative, wrote, "My good friend Steve McVey has put the amazing back into grace."

❖ Bestselling author Gary Smalley said, "Few people have had the life change effect on my life that Steve McVey has had. Whenever I hear that he has a new book, I buy several copies."

❖ Neil Anderson, author of *The Bondage Breaker*: "(Steve McVey's book) *A Divine Invitation* will enlarge your heart and increase your comprehension of God's love that goes beyond knowledge."

❖ The late Bill Bright, founder of Campus Crusade for Christ, wrote about *A Divine Invitation*: "Steve McVey has given us in very clear and understandable language a wonderful, indelible picture of just how beautiful, complete and even startling God's love for us really is."

Steve McVey writes to address specific needs in the reader's life. His books are filled with biblical truth, practical application, humor and affirmation that will encourage you and strengthen you in your own journey of faith. Buy just one of his books today and, like those who have written their reviews above, you will find yourself wanting to buy all of McVey's books.

There is plenty of religious jargon out there on the market. These books will talk about your life, the things you face, and how the grace of God will guide you safely through them and enrich your life in the process.

(R)
Target (L) on 124
Next Light (R) on
R. Razen to Pl Hill
→ 85 (L) S.

50600833R00078

Made in the USA
Lexington, KY
22 March 2016